Praise for
The Abundance Tree

"If you want to go beyond dreaming your
dream to LIVING your dream, I highly
recommend this book."

—John-Roger
New York Times #1 bestselling author

The Abundance Tree

The Abundance Tree

A Simple Handbook for Growing Your Dreams

Patricia Heyman

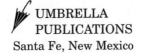

UMBRELLA
PUBLICATIONS
Santa Fe, New Mexico

Published by:
Umbrella Publications
PO Box 6817
Santa Fe, NM 87502

Edited by Ellen Kleiner
Book design by Mary Shapiro
Back cover photo by Niels Leppert
Cover illustration by Ingrid Kelley
Illustrations by Janice St. Marie

PUBLISHER'S CATALOGING-IN-PUBLICATION
Heyman, Patricia.
The abundance tree: a simple handbook for growing your
dreams/Patricia Heyman.—1st ed.
p. cm.
Preassigned LCCN: 97-61533
ISBN 0-9659332-0-2:
1. Success—Psychological aspects. 2. Risk-taking (Psychology)
3. Gratitude. I. Title.
BF637.S8H49 1997   158.1
                                QBI97-41047

This book is dedicated to my friend and teacher John-Roger, whose work has inspired me and others to fulfill our potential for true abundance and liberation.

Acknowledgments

I extend grateful acknowledgment to the Insight Seminars, where I have developed the knowledge and experience base to create this handbook.

I thank my husband Stan and sons Jason and Mark, whose love and support have nurtured and sustained me.

Thanks also to John Roesler for asking me to write this book.

Contents

Preface

This handbook contains many of the primary laws of manifestation made easy. They spring to life through the image of the Abundance Tree—a healthy, fruit-bearing tree that grows stronger and more beautiful with each passing season.

The Abundance Tree is a metaphor for any of our dreams, be they about money, joy, love, or success. I chose the image of a tree because of the adage I heard as a child that "money doesn't grow on trees." On the East Coast where I was raised, trees were plentiful—exhibiting strength, beauty, and ever-growing abundance—but money was not. As a result, I developed some limiting views of money and abundance. Creating what I wanted in my life seemed possible only with hard work, and I did not trust that prosperity of any sort could flow easily.

Many of us live in a similar mind-set of lack. Yet sources as ancient as the Old Testament and as recent as the writings of Deepak Chopra, MD, tell us that we are meant to be prosperous and that abundance is everywhere. This simple book is dedicated to the proposition that we are in charge of our lives and that the universe is present and ready to give in proportion to our willingness to receive.

Introduction

Do you have what you really want? Do you wake up each day knowing there is an Abundance Tree in your life, or is it still waiting to be planted, or perhaps nurtured?

According to the premise of this book, if you have a strong intention, the results will show up in your life. Conversely, if you see no results, then limiting beliefs of one sort or another are coloring that desire. In other words, if you don't have what you think you want right now, then something is keeping you from it. Either a lack of clarity or some limiting idea in which you are invested is preventing you from realizing the intention you profess to have.

The first step in creating what you want is to define what it is—as clearly and precisely as possible. When you envision abundance, what do you picture?

The definition of abundance, according to *Merriam-Webster's Collegiate Dictionary,* is:

1. an extremely plentiful or oversufficient quantity or supply; 2. affluence, wealth; 3. overflowing fullness: abundance of the heart.

What is *your* definition? What does it mean to you to be abundant, or prosperous?

Do you want:

To be wealthy, in possession of more than enough money?

To be happy?

To be joyful?

To have plenty of love and sex?

To have children?

To have healthy, rewarding relationships?

To have a good job in a profession you love?

To be creative and help manifest visions for yourself and your family?

To provide for your family?

To educate yourself (and your children)?

To travel extensively?

To be physically healthy?

To feel spiritually nourished?

List your desires. Then focus in on the abundance you want to go for *now*. And remember, be specific.

Your definition of abundance will move you out of the realm of fantasy by grounding your abstract desire for prosperity in concrete realities, by anchoring your intention in solid goals. Before, you may have wanted abundance. Now, you know what that *means*. With this knowledge, you can effectively sow the seeds of your dreams.

Chapter 1

Nourishing the Roots of Prosperity

Let's say you've planted a seed for the tree called Abundance but after a while it fails to grow. Despite the clarity of your intention, the tree begins to wither.

Why do we strive and strive and still not get results? What causes us to miss the mark?

Often the problem can be found in the seedbed. If the soil is parched, contaminated, or lacking in certain nutrients, a tree cannot grow to its full potential.

The Abundance Tree takes root in the soil of belief systems and past experiences. Sometimes the beliefs handed down from generation to generation are nourishing. Often, however, they are too negative to support anything more than a sapling. Here are some limiting beliefs about money:

"Money is the root of all evil."

"You can't take your money with you."

"A fool and his money are soon parted."

"Money is too much responsibility."

"It takes money to make money."

"Money is dirty."

"She is *filthy* rich."

Our childhood experiences, too, have given rise to a system of survival, part of which has outlived its usefulness. For example, think of all the times you've told yourself:

"I'm not good enough."

"I don't deserve it."

"I don't have the ability to do it."

"If I have a lot, someone will go without."

"I go without because you have too much."

"There isn't enough to go around."

"People are greedy."

"One has to work hard for one's money."

By the same token, have you ever spent so much time reviewing options that the moment for action passed on by? If so, a lack of trust emerging after a letdown in childhood may have led you to mistrust this opportunity.

Antiquated dynamics keep us locked in old self-defeating patterns. But just as the earth can be cultivated, so can our perceptions expand into a larger and more effective worldview.

The best way for this to occur is to let the old beliefs and experiences become fertilizer for personal growth. Negative and outmoded assumptions, in other words, can become fodder for the roots of your Abundance Tree.

How can you transform the limiting beliefs and negative messages that are sabotaging your efforts to achieve prosperity? First, name them and write them on a sheet of paper. Then burn it. Finally, mix the ashes into the soil that feeds your dreams. Value these ashes for what they are—namely, a means for creating new reference points for more abundant and joyful life patterns!

When the residue of old limiting beliefs is turned back into the soil, your Abundance Tree will begin to establish a healthy, secure root system. The trunk will rise steadily out of the earth, because the roots will be sustained by a soil alive with discovery, acceptance, and change.

Chapter 2

Turning Stumbling Blocks into Stepping Stones

Rocky soil, too, can impair the growth of the Abundance Tree, but only if its roots lack strength and resilience. If its roots are hardy, they will grow around each rock they encounter. In fact, with every obstruction they overcome, their strength and flexibility will increase.

The same sort of growth can unfold when *you* get to a tough spot. You can cross the hurdle and, in the process, grow stronger and more pliant.

We are able to grow in spite of—and often because of—the obstacles we encounter. Why? Because bumping up against a stone prompts us to exert extra strength and creativity. With continued movement, we become propelled by new surges of energy that push us around the hurdle, or even through it.

Once we are on the other side, our circumstances tend to improve. Losing a job may inspire us to take a better one. Running out of money may show us how resourceful we really are.

In the end we discover that each stone holds a valuable lesson.

Attitude counts. If your approach is "I never get what I want" or "I knew this would be too hard," the stumbling blocks may remain stumbling blocks. But if you clarify your intention and visualize the outcome you desire, original methods for achieving it will soon show up.

Confidence, in both yourself and your intention, is critical. To build confidence, listen to feedback from the universe—loved ones, friends, associates, and others in your immediate environment—and observe the results of your actions.

Openness to new perspectives paves the way. Just as the tree that bends in the breeze is able to endure a storm, responding to environmental stimuli will keep you resilient enough to express an intention creatively.

These three qualities help us turn stumbling blocks into stepping stones. Fortified with a positive attitude, confidence, and openness, we can greet each rock in life as an occasion for developing strength and stepping upward.

There are three kinds of people in the world:

> Those who make things happen
> Those who watch things happen
> Those who wonder what happened.

The people in the third group are the victims.

We have all felt like victims at some point in our lives. Many of us even see ourselves as victims of good fortune, as if we had nothing to do with the blessings that "came our way." This perception of being "acted upon"—for good or for ill—is disempowering.

To move through obstruction, we need only look at the roles we played in our past successes as well as our failures. Often we examine only the failures. Remembering our contributions to success, however, can awaken visions and goals, illuminating our true purpose in life.

If you have trouble acknowledging your accountability in successful outcomes, do this exercise:

Look back at a successful event in your life—a business venture, perhaps, or a relationship or career shift. Identify the point at which it began, as well as the many "choice points" you encountered along the way.

Ask yourself, "Which choice did I make at each of these junctures?" Then reflect on what you wanted at the outset and on the strength of your intention. Were you willing to do whatever was needed to achieve your goal?

What happens when you go after a dream with *commitment?*

Personal accountability in negative situations is sometimes harder to see. To gain perspective on this, try asking yourself, **"Were there warning signs that I missed?" or "Imagining that I had no options, did I overlook viable choices?"**

Every large project entails a series of small steps, many of which are measurable. So if you should stumble, or even fall, after setting forth on a new undertaking, review the victories and downfalls of the past. Then bring this information into your present experience and mount the steps one by one.

Chapter 3

Intention versus Method

Many of us are taught that to get what we want we must first figure out a method for achieving it. Arriving at methods too soon, however, can restrict the outcome.

A more fruitful approach is to model ourselves after the Abundance Tree, which aspires to reach toward the sky by fulfilling its potential, by becoming the macrocosm of its microcosmic seed. That is its purpose.

As humans, we begin with the seed of an idea. Within this seed are all the elements needed to bring the idea to fruition. Like the seed of the tree, it needs sunlight (clear statements), water (nourishing support), and fertilizer (steps forward) to keep the original intention active.

The following incidents illustrate the power of an intention at work:

Example 1. I direct a seminar company in the Southwest. It began as a branch office of a large seminar company that was presenting worldwide. Located in a midsize town, our branch was viewed as temporary, at best. Those who worked there, however, had a vision: to develop a center for seminars throughout the region. Committed to our dream, we brainstormed and created seminars that were so well attended they soon became prototypes adopted by branches nationwide.

We continued to grow, and three years after our inception, we became independent. Again the success of our efforts defied all odds. Now, five years later, we present seminars in a large metropolitan area nearby and in two neighboring states. Moreover, we have created new seminars, found additional topics to investigate, and developed a business division. All along, the vision has held steady.

Example 2. All my life I have wanted to travel. Each time I envisioned a new place—in Europe, the Middle East, Russia, Hawaii, the South Seas—I focused my intention on going there, having no idea how I'd actually set forth. Over time, this promise to myself remained strong, and methods soon showed up. With surprising boosts from the universe, I have managed to visit all these destinations and more.

Example 3. Then there was the time my family needed a larger house. We were renting and hoped to purchase a new home, but had no cash for a down payment. We began imagining the type of house we wanted, the number of rooms it would have, the part of town it would be in. Then we took the logical next steps: we called a real estate agent, looked at houses, and began asking for money.

After that came the surprise—our landlord called and insisted that we buy our rental or move out. The pressure was on: we didn't want the rental and had no idea what to do. At last we met a couple who were about to put their house on the market. When we went to see it, they said they had already had an offer. Twenty-four hours later we made them an offer of our own and gave them some earnest money, still having no clue where the purchase money would come from. In the two-month interval before our scheduled closing, we received a substantial amount of unexpected income, making it possible for us to secure the down payment and cover the closing costs of the purchase. From start to finish, the project took four months, each week of which brought us closer to our vision.

You, too, can transform fantasies
into realities by remaining true
to your intentions. Simply be willing to
accept assistance in whatever form it
arises and keep moving in the
direction in which you want to go.

Chapter 4

Risk Taking

"Come to the edge."
"We can't. We will fall."
"Come to the edge."
"We can't! We are afraid!"

And they came.
And he pushed them.
And they flew.

—Guillaume Apollinaire

The Abundance Tree, like all trees, takes risks as it grows. To develop, it must reach for the light of the sun; yet the taller it grows, the more likely it is to be cut down.

Like the tree that rises out of the darkness of the earth, we emerge from the womb of mediocrity and status quo, and with us comes a vision of something new. Do we risk moving toward it or do we cling to our old behaviors and beliefs?

The refusal to change will keep us right where we are. Some put it this way: "If you always do what you've always done, you'll always get what you've always gotten."

When we continue our old patterns *hoping* for a change, we often begin to feel ineffective, if not crazy. One definition of insanity is, doing things the same way as before and expecting different results.

All growth entails risk. Yet much as we may profess to want growth, we are sometimes reluctant to take the gamble. Why? Because we are afraid of the unknown, or because we feel guilty about past mistakes.

Overcoming Fear

When the refusal to change is rooted in fear of the unknown, we are governed by a desire to be safe from harm. We are afraid of being hurt or of losing everything we are used to having.

What, really, is fear? One way to conceive of it is by considering this acronym:

F—fantasy
E—expectations
A—appearing
R—real

The fear is real; the object of the fear is not. For example, if you are afraid of losing all your money, the fear you feel is genuine, but the loss of money is an illusion, because it hasn't happened.

As we begin changing our belief systems, we need to be mindful of the "little kid" part of us who is afraid, who holds dearly to earlier impressions still appearing as truths. Caring for yourself during this time of risk is essential. Acknowledge yourself for all the positive steps you are taking as you risk new behaviors and experiences.

Another tool helpful in fostering this transition is visualization. Picture yourself pursuing your dream and doing it perfectly. Look at as many details in the scene as possible. While watching yourself in action, silently repeat the phrase "For the highest good." This message will allow for the emergence of unanticipated benefits.

The tree is safe from harm as long as it stays underground, sequestered away from warmth and light. As soon as it begins propelling itself toward the sun, however, it gives up this safety. Venturing forth to fulfill the potential contained within its seed, the tree is supported by the fertility of the soil.

We give up our safety with strong doses of self-support and acknowledgment. These ingredients provide the energy for our continued growth.

Supporting ourselves as we step forward also requires a working knowledge of the self—or as John-Roger calls it in his book *The Dynamics of the Lower Self,* the "three selves," namely, the High Self, the Conscious Self, and the Basic Self. Despite their names, none of these selves is more important than any other.

Indeed, each one plays a vital role in bringing our dreams to fruition:

The *High Self* is responsible for our inspiration and visions. It has an overview of our life and our place in the world.

The *Conscious Self* is made up of our learned behaviors and beliefs. It reasons, thinks, and evaluates our experiences as well as those of others.

The *Basic Self* is the seat of instincts, emotions, and bodily functioning. It operates much like a four- or five-year-old child, keeping us aware of our physical needs for food, sleep, elimination; our sexual feelings; and our emotions. It is literal, like a computer, and it provides the energy for our accomplishments.

Changing our limiting beliefs while feeding new, affirmative beliefs into the Basic and Conscious Selves creates a new consciousness. The acknowledgment we give ourselves nourishes this new consciousness, much as the rain, soil, and sunlight feed the sprouting tree.

With the care and feeding of the self under way, it is time to commit to the dream. To *commit* is to take the first step rather than think about it. When we are committed, the universe moves to assist us in ways we may never have dreamed possible.

Remember, the universe rewards action, not thought. So step forward, then see what happens.

Until one is committed,
there is hesitancy,
the chance to draw back,
always ineffectiveness.
Concerning all acts
of initiative (and creation)
there is one elementary truth,
the ignorance of which kills
countless ideas and splendid plans:
that the moment
one definitely commits oneself,
then Providence moves too.
All sorts of things occur
to help one that would never
otherwise have occurred.
A whole stream of events
issues from the decision,
raising in one's favor all manner
of unforeseen incidents and meetings
and material assistance,
which no one man could have dreamed
would have come his way.

—W. H. Murray
The Scottish Himalayan Expedition

Whatever you can do,
or dream you can, begin it.
Boldness has genius,
power and magic in it.

—Goethe

Overcoming Guilt

When we feel guilty about past mistakes, we are reluctant to take risks for fear that doing so will prompt more mistakes. To surmount our guilt we must first examine its origins.

Guilt occurs when our actions conflict with the image we have of ourselves. Experiencing this conflict, we may sacrifice everything to be "right," or focus rigidly on defending our position. Another option is to let go of the need to be right and replace it with the need to simply "be."

Mistakes arise when we proceed with insufficient information. Yet how are we to obtain information without venturing forth and learning from our experiences? Therein lies the irony of guilt-ridden decisions.

It makes no sense to beat ourselves up for making mistakes. Instead, we must keep going, changing our course when necessary, and recognizing that the universe will show us which path to follow.

Remember, guilt keeps us protecting
a self-image that does not allow for
imperfections. As humans, however,
we seek excellence, not perfection!

Consider the following account from a man unwilling to risk a business venture because he is burdened with guilt over a mistake he made five years earlier. His statements of action follow; the image he is striving to protect is defined below them.

Action
"I started a business five years ago.
I invested my savings.
The market for my product was saturated; and I did not know there were cheaper, more efficient ways to manufacture it.
I lost the business and spent several years paying back investors."

G   U   I   L   T

Image
I am an intelligent person.
I am a good businessperson.
I am responsible and caring.
I am trustworthy.

This man's perception of himself, which he is struggling to preserve, rings true to those who know him. And yet it is not reflected in his actions! The wall of guilt he has erected to safeguard his self-image is holding him back from a potentially successful undertaking.

A wall of guilt does protect one's self-image, but it also feels lousy. It has a paralyzing effect, causing physical discomforts and, at times, disease. The trick is to find a way to live with past events *without feeling guilty.*

How can this man eradicate the guilt he is carrying? He would have to change either the *action* or the *image*.

Can he alter the action? No, because it has already transpired. Can he change the image? Yes. Does he need to discard portions of it? No, for they are all true. He could, however, expand it to encompass his human flaws and the learning they inspire.

He could modify his image by adding one or more of the following statements:

"I have learned that more market research is sometimes necessary."

"I don't always ask for assistance when I ought to."

"When I make a mistake, I take responsibility for my actions."

"I sometimes miscalculate, especially when I need more information."

"I have some of the information I need."

You, too, can eradicate guilt by modifying the image you seek to uphold. Expanding that image to encompass *growth* and *learning* will help you give up the need to be right.

After all, would you rather be right or happy?

Chapter 5

Letting Go of Mediocrity

What do human beings resist the most?
Change.
Why?
Because we like to feel comfortable.

We live in a comfort zone made up of all that is familiar, including people, places, work habits, and experiences.

When we approach the edge of our comfort zone, we get uncomfortable—a state we associate with fear. Although we may not enjoy all the familiar aspects of our existence, the desire to avoid discomfort keeps us within the zone, within the confines of the mediocre. We even erect an imaginary barrier around it.

Drawn strongly to an experience outside the comfort zone, however, we find the resources needed to help us push through this barrier. And each time we cross it, it stretches, enlarging the zone to accommodate the new experience.

So it is that when we take risks, our comfort zone expands, allowing us to step farther and farther out and experience more of life.

Here are some tips for breaking out of the comfort zone:

- Make a decision to move toward the goal or experience you desire.
- Lean into the process by taking the first step.
- Observe feedback from the universe to see if you are on course. If you are off course, make a new decision.

Only by moving can we tell if we are headed in the right direction. If we are not, we can simply reroute ourselves, without regret or self-flagellation.

Checking in with the universe is nothing new. You probably do it every day, unaware that the universe is set up to support you and that it is constantly providing feedback on how you are doing.

How often have you exclaimed in exasperation:

"I can't do anything right," or
"Bitch, bitch, bitch. All you ever do is criticize me"!

In those moments you were responding to feedback from the universe. But you were taking the feedback personally, as though it were assessing your worthiness as a human being. In reality, it was merely *providing information,* letting you know you were off course.

Breaking through the barrier of the comfort zone is like the ever-radiating root activity of the Abundance Tree. Roots, especially when well fertilized, will push beyond the radius of the trunk, forming the basis for long, leafy branches of fruit.

The message of the fertilizer is:
Keep moving.

The message of the push beyond the comfort zone is:
Keep moving. Worthiness has to do with who you are, not what you do.

Chapter 6

Self-Talk

How many times a day do you talk to yourself in a negative manner, or picture your actions resulting in a negative outcome?

Negative affirmations are usually by-products of worry.

Anxious, we may mutter to ourselves:

> "Boy, I'm stupid."
> "I can't believe what a screwup I am."
> "I can't do it."
> "I'm not good at that."
> "I'm a failure."
> "I'll never get it right."

Or we may think:

> I don't have enough time.
> They don't like me.
> I'm not good enough.
> That won't work.
> I'm too confused.

Negative affirmations divert the energy flowing toward a goal. They can even para-lyze all progress and, like the serpent hairs on Medusa's head, turn everything in sight to stone.

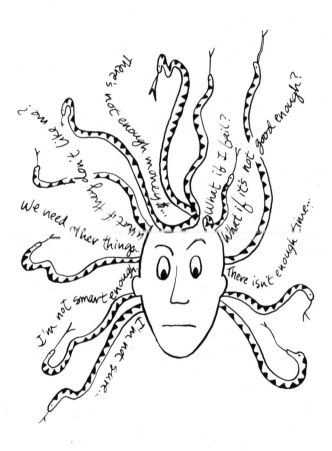

So become conscious of the negative messages you send yourself. To overcome the paralysis they cause, follow them up with uplifting messages stated in the present tense. These positive affirmations will get your energy moving once again, straight through the limiting beliefs.

Most of us have limiting beliefs about money. Sometimes these are experienced inwardly as vague doubts or inexplicable anger about currency, price tags, or wealthy people. Other times, they come to expression. When they do, we can work with them.

On the following pages are two clearly articulated limiting beliefs about money, together with positive affirmations that can move the goal-directed energy back on course.

Limiting belief #1. If I were to make a lot of money, I'd just fritter it away. I don't know how to invest well, so I'm sure the money would disappear or someone would take it from me.

Affirmation A. I have more than enough money in my life, and I am handling it well.

Affirmation B. I am experiencing great wealth, and I am distributing it with intelligence and integrity. I now have all the information I need to make wise, thoughtful investments. I am enjoying my money and using it well.

Limiting belief #2. Pure is pure. If I were wealthy, I'd be snobbish and would stop caring about my friends.

Affirmation A. I have achieved my goal of wealth, and I am using it generously.

Affirmation B. I am enjoying more than enough money in my life, using it wisely, and donating freely to causes that are important to me.

If you are attempting to make more money but it does not seem to be coming your way, list your limiting beliefs about money. Then create positive affirmations in the present tense. Finally, *visualize the outcome you want.* Include as many details as you can.

The first step in visualization is to train yourself to stay with the fantasy of the goal you have in mind. If negative thoughts enter the picture, write them down and burn them, or simply reconstruct the image.

The visualization will serve as your *intention* as you lean in the direction of your goal.

Negative self-talk affects not only our finances but our relationships. If you are attempting to attract more friends or iron out difficulties in an important relationship, and nothing seems to work:

- List your limiting beliefs about relationships.
- Compose positive affirmations in the present tense to reinvigorate your efforts.
- Visualize the outcome you want.

Treat every day as the first day of the rest of your life. Leave no room for regrets. Remember, all your experiences have contributed to who you are right now. If you don't have what you want, use the three-step method described above.

What do you want? Once you know what it is, here's how you can get it:

- **Ask for it.**
- **Give it away.**
- **Take charge**—don't wait for someone else to.
- **Fake it till you make it.** The mind can play with this process, especially if it is used to hearing negative self-talk. It may respond with, "I know this is not true!" How does it know? It doesn't—it is just thinking it does and is closing down to new information. So fake it, all the while feeding your mind with new infor- mation to fill in the blanks and color the scene.
- **Break down the route to your destination into individual steps.** As you take each one, remain alert to infor- mation coming your way. That's your feedback!
- **Give up the need to be right.** Change course when necessary, contin- ually keeping the final goal in mind.

Chapter 7

Gratitude

Once the Abundance Tree is exposed to excessive sunlight or wind, it runs the risk of misfortune. It is able to withstand the adversity, however, because it is endowed with an inner strength. For us, this inner strength arises from gratitude—a state of joyous thankfulness.

To assess your capacity to withstand adversity, do this experiment:

- Thinking back over the previous twenty-four hours, count the number of times you bemoaned what went wrong, or what was missing.
- Tally the number of times you acknowledged what went right and what was there for you.

Chances are that you did more bemoaning than acknowledging. If so, it is time to train your mind to focus on gratitude.

Begin by expressing thanks twice each day for the positive features in your life. Say, for example:

"I am grateful for my physical health."

"I am grateful for the love of my children."

"I am grateful for the warmth of my house."

"I am grateful for the success of my business."

"I am grateful for my paycheck."

"I am grateful to have come this far in my life."

"I am grateful for my friends."

"I am grateful for my partner."

"I am grateful for my abundance."

As time passes, you will begin to naturally acknowledge the plusses in your life. Whenever negative thinking enters into your thoughts, you will be able to refocus them because you will have developed an ***attitude of gratitude.***

Remember, you can get what you focus on. To see how this works, imagine a walk in the woods amid towering trees, flashes of sunlight, fresh air, and perfect temperatures. Suddenly, you notice a pile of horse manure, then another one, and yet another. You have two choices: to ignore the piles and focus on the beauty around you, or to focus on the piles and forget the beauty.

Focus on the beauty! Why? Because what you see is what you get.

If you see the beauty, that is what you will come away with. And that is what you will be grateful for.

Your attitude of gratitude will nourish your dreams. Soon you will discover that *if you want what you have, you'll have what you want.*

Chapter 8

Keeping Active As You Pursue Your Dreams

The Abundance Tree goes through seasonal changes as it matures. With each passing season comes a new growth pattern, all of which contribute to the completion of its mission. So it is that any time we set our sights on fulfilling a dream, the project undergoes a "cycle of performance," as does each of its stages.

The cycle of performance mimics the seasons of the year. Knowing where we are each day on our journey through this cycle helps us direct our energy most efficiently as we bring a dream to fruition. To maintain momentum, we must actively engage in each phase of the cycle.

The Cycle of Performance

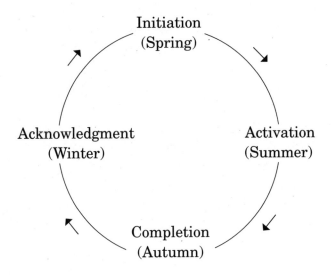

Initiation
(Spring)

Activation
(Summer)

Completion
(Autumn)

Acknowledgment
(Winter)

While pursuing a dream, we often fool ourselves into believing we are physically moving forward when in fact we are suspended in thoughts and fantasies. The way to proceed is by leaning into the path of the dream by taking an action step. If all goes well, we take the next step and again attend to the feedback. Remember, *the absence of feedback is feedback.*

We can always change course when the road we are on does not lead to our destination. The point is that most learning occurs when we venture out into new territory. *The universe rewards action, not thought.*

Spring (Initiation)

When you begin a project, be sure to push energetically away from inertia. To grow from seed to seedling, your project will need the water of acknowledgment, the inner nourishment of gratitude, and the fertilizer of your transformed limiting beliefs. It will also require unique perspectives and new input. This is the time to develop your intention and to choose the most promising methods for proceeding.

Spring—a season rich with fertility—is the period for moving forward. So talk to people, test out new ideas, welcome the feedback you receive. Be on the lookout for new life, original points of view, and fresh information. Soon you will see the object of your dream pushing into the light of day, complete with the first buds of success.

To sustain the process, select a series of actions geared for an ESI (external focus–support–internal focus) accomplishment. For each one, jot down:

- The *external focus,* or goal, you wish to achieve.
- The forms of *support* you will need to attain this goal, such as collaboration, information, assistance, or creative expression. The more help you have, the better. Remember, support means that you do it yourself but not by yourself.
- The positive and realistic *internal focus* you plan to turn to when self-doubts or limiting beliefs crop up. The internal focus may be a realistic vision of the future, positive affirmations, or visualizations. As a preventive measure, take time each day to concentrate on your internal focus. This discipline will help ward off the inclination to entertain negative outcomes, or to say, "What if _____" or "I'm scared that _____ will happen."

Here is a sample entry for an ESI accomplishment.

External focus:
I will increase my business by 25 percent over the next three months.

Support:
A business consultant
People with similar businesses
Staff training for more effective productivity
Including staff in decision making and creative solutions
Creative and playful innovations
Community outreach

Internal focus:
Each day I will visualize the telephone ringing more frequently with inquiries about our product. The callers will be interested in our product and will place orders. They will be pleased with our services and will tell their friends and acquaintances about us. I will see myself enjoying the fruits of the increased income—new office furniture, an additional employee, upgraded equipment, a week-long vacation in Bali.

Summer (Activation)

The focus now is on doing rather than initiating. Set all your plans in motion and see how they work. Are the fresh nutrients feeding the roots of your endeavor? Is the Abundance Tree getting taller and growing leafy branches? Is its trunk stronger than ever? Continue fertilizing with the limiting beliefs you have exchanged for more expansive ones, watering with the acknowledgment of the goals you have accomplished, and furnishing the inner nourishment of gratitude.

In summer the Abundance Tree does most of its growing. The days are long and warm, allowing for an increased absorption of sunlight and earth-borne nutrients. Many of your plans will come to fruition. Acknowledging their completion will energize those that are still in process.

Some of these plans may need revising. Those that do will let you know by either withering or failing to yield results. Let this be a call for flexibility, rather than regret. Remember, the willow that bends in the breeze is sturdy enough to withstand a variety of challenges.

Autumn (Completion)

Displays of glorious autumn foliage stand as testimony to the beauty of a completed cycle. In the cycle of nature, the fruit is now harvested and portions of summer's growth are discarded to prepare for the root expansion of winter. In the cycle of performance, certain aspects of the dream have been fulfilled whereas others will move forward. The game plan may shift, yet the goal, adhered to with focused intention, will remain the same.

The air is crisp, brimming with a new energy of acceptance. Bask in your achievements. Determine which plans to keep and which ones to surrender. Honor not only the triumphs but the mistakes, for they too have contributed to your understanding.

Winter (Acknowledgment)

The growth in winter occurs invisibly—in deeply probing roots beneath the surface of the earth and in the vascular system within the trunks of trees. Although the Abundance Tree may appear to be asleep, it is actually teeming with life in preparation for a new spring. This is a time for increasingly creative thought and for checking out the universe's responses to the steps you have taken.

Acknowledge all your plans that have come to fruition. Why? Because the acknowledgment you give will permeate the roots of your project, providing energy for the start of a new cycle on the spiral of abundance.

Chapter 9

Reaching Your Long-term Goals

To come to fruition, many dreams require long-term planning. These are best approached through a series of short-term steps.

To begin, decide on a goal you can accomplish within a year; when the year is up, you can plan the next phase of the project. Next, divide the yearly goal into monthly goals. On a week-by-week basis, you will be breaking these down into weekly goals. This strategy, although seemingly artificial, will bolster you with the rewards of several completion cycles, providing energy and enthusiasm for continuing.

Remember, a journey of
a thousand miles begins with
a small stride forward
and continues one step at a time.

goal achieved!

DIPLOMA

support system

reward system

getting information

CAFE
OPEN 24 HRS
OPEN

positive visualization

making time

How to Proceed

At the beginning of each week, identify up to ten goals, or steps you wish to take, for that week. Set a date of completion for each one. At the end of the week:

- See which steps you have mastered.
- Acknowledge their completion.
- Share your successes.
- Celebrate—go someplace special, bathe by candlelight, buy yourself a gift, treat yourself to a dinner out, a hike in the woods, or a day in the country.
- Formulate new steps for the week to come. Avoid dwelling on any unaccomplished goals; instead, either add them to your new list or set them aside for the future.

This nuts-and-bolts approach will engage the practical side of you in endeavors to keep the action going as your more conceptual side continues to work with focused intention, affirmations, and visualizations. Remain open to new information capable of moving you either further in the same direction or off into an even more exciting one.

Stepping Lightly

Angels fly because they take themselves lightly. And so can you.

Avoid awfulizing, catastrophizing, and thinking ponderously. These will only drag you down. If you must think, draw a mind map to help you brainstorm expansively.

NEW JOB
with better pay and
more fulfilling work

JOB OFFER*

INTERVIEWS

PREPARE

CALL TO FOLLOW UP

SEND RESUME

DONE PROFESSIONALLY

HAVE RESUME

ASK FOR SUGGESTIONS

JOB OFFER

SET UP INTERVIEWS

PREPARE AN UP-TO-DATE RESUME

ASK HOW THEY DID IT

INTERVIEW OTHERS IN THE SAME FIELD

PREPARE OUTFIT FOR INTERVIEW

CALL POSSIBILITIES

CHECK NEWSPAPERS

CLEAR OUT CLOTHES CLOSET

SEND RESUME

GO TO JOB FAIRS WITH AVAILABLE JOBS

MAKE APPTS FOR INTERVIEWS

JOB OFFER

CREATE AFFIRMATION

SAY AFFIRMATION DAILY

CREATE A VISUALIZATION OF IDEAL SCENE

VISUALIZE DAILY

WRITE DOWN LIMITING BELIEFS ABOUT SUCCESS

BURN BELIEFS

Above all, keep your sense of humor.

■ Step back and view life as a flowing stream that integrates mistakes and missteps into its current.
■ Be willing to laugh with yourself.
■ See the mirror image in everything you observe about others and the situations around you.
■ Laugh every day! Cry if you need to, and move on.

The Abundance Tree draws nourishment from its roots as it reaches toward the sky. So may you acknowledge the past yet live in the present.

Count your blessings, and use the bounty in the world for your unfolding, knowing that it is all here for you.

Recommended Reading

A Whack on the Side of the Head, by Roger
von Oech, illustrated by George Willett
(New York: Warner Books, 1990)

Life 101 Series, by John-Roger and Peter
McWilliams (Los Angeles: Prelude Press):
Do It! (1991)
Life 101 (1991)
Wealth 101 (1992)
*You Can't Afford the Luxury of a
Negative Thought* (1991)

Wealth and Higher Consciousness, by
John-Roger (Los Angeles: Mandeville
Press, 1988)

About the Author

Patricia Heyman, MSW, LISW, is a facilitator of Insight Seminars and president of the Life Education Network of the Southwest (LENS), a nonprofit seminar company dedicated to personal fulfillment and world harmony. Creator and presenter of a variety of seminars worldwide, she is the originator of experiential workshops on sex, relationships and intimacy, as well as abundance and gratitude.

Patricia has been a facilitator, counselor, educator, and consultant for thirty years. In addition to working with community programs as well as businesses, she has chaired the Counseling Department of Southwestern College, where she developed a professional curriculum to advance the teaching of counseling into the twenty-first century.

Married and the mother of two sons, Patricia makes her home in Santa Fe, New Mexico. A dynamic presenter, she has helped thousands of people discover abundance and joy as a way of life through her wisdom, clarity, humor, and gentle surgery for the heart.

Ordering Information

Quantity	Amount
_____ x $11.95 per book	_____
Sales tax of 6.25% (for NM residents)	_____
Shipping & handling ($2.70; plus $1.00 per book on orders of two or more)	_____
Total amount enclosed	_____

Quantity discounts available

_____

Name

_____

Address

_____

City   State   Zip

Method of payment
❑ check or money order enclosed
❑ MasterCard   ❑ Visa

☐☐☐☐ ☐☐☐☐ ☐☐☐☐ ☐☐☐☐

_____

Signature   exp. date

Please photocopy this order form, fill it out,
and mail it, together with check, money order,
or charge-card information, to:

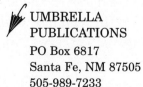 UMBRELLA
PUBLICATIONS
PO Box 6817
Santa Fe, NM 87505
505-989-7233